AF898691

HORSE FARM

SHETLAND PONIES

ANNE ACCARDI

NorwoodHouse Press

Cataloging-in-Publication Data

Names: Accardi, Anne.
Title: Shetland ponies / Anne Accardi.
Description: Buffalo, NY : Norwood House Press, 2027. | Series: Horse farm | Includes glossary and index.
Identifiers: ISBN 9781978580893 (pbk.) | ISBN 9781978580909 (library bound) | ISBN 9781978580916 (ebook)
Subjects: LCSH: Shetland pony--Juvenile literature.
Classification: LCC SF315.2.S5 A33 2027 | DDC 636.16--dc23

Published in 2027 by
Norwood House Press
2544 Clinton Street
Buffalo, NY 14224

Copyright © 2027 Norwood House Press
Designer: Rhea Magaro
Editor: Kim Thompson

Photo credits: Cover, pp. 1, 7, 8, 11, 14, 21 Rita_Kochmarjova/Shutterstock.com; p. 5 FamVeld/Shutterstock.com; p. 6 Wikipedia; p. 9 Nonthachai Saksri/Shutterstock.com; p. 10 Annabell Gsoedl/Shutterstock.com; p. 13 kezza/Shutterstock.com; p. 15 Martin Charles Hatch/Shutterstock.com; p. 17 TW27/Shutterstock.com; p. 18 Bariso/Shutterstock.com; p. 19 Dusan Petkovic/Shutterstock.com;

All rights reserved. No part of this book may be reproduced in any form without permission in writing from the publisher, except by a reviewer.

Printed in the United States of America

Some of the images in this book illustrate individuals who are models. The depictions do not imply actual situations or events.

CPSIA compliance information: Batch #CSNHP27: For further information contact Norwood House Press at 1-800-237-9932.

Find us on

TABLE OF CONTENTS

Meet the Shetland Pony....................4
What Do Shetland Ponies Look Like?....................8
How Do Shetland Ponies Help People?....................12
What Do Shetland Ponies Need?....................18
Glossary....................22
Thinking Questions....................23
Index....................24
About the Author....................24

Meet the Shetland Pony

The Shetland **pony** is a popular horse **breed**. Kids love to ride these little horses!

Shetland ponies have been around for thousands of years. They come from the Shetland Islands in Scotland.

The islands are cold and snowy.

What Do Shetland Ponies Look Like?

Shetland ponies have short legs and small heads. Their bodies are **compact**.

These horses are strong and **muscular**.

They are small but mighty!

Shetland ponies are **hardy**. Their heavy **coats** keep them warm.

They can be any color. Some have white marks on their heads and legs.

How Do Shetland Ponies Help People?

Shetland ponies are great workers.

They can **haul** heavy loads.

Long ago, they pulled plows on farms.

They pulled carts in mines.

These ponies can be **stubborn**. But they are usually friendly.

They are used at petting zoos and carnivals. Even little kids can ride them.

Some people keep Shetland ponies as pets.

They are good helpers. They can lead people who are blind.

What Do Shetland Ponies Need?

Shetland ponies do not need much food. They mostly eat **hay**.

Their shaggy manes should be **groomed** often.

Shetland ponies need lots of exercise.

These animals are very **social**. They love being with other horses!

Glossary

breed (breed): one type or kind of an animal

coats (kohts): hair or fur that covers animals' bodies

compact (kahm-PAKT): packed together in a small space; dense

groomed (groomd): combed, brushed, and cleaned

hardy (HAHR-dee): strong and healthy; able to survive in harsh conditions

haul (hawl): to pull or drag

hay (hay): long grass that is cut, dried, and used as food for farm animals

muscular (MUHS-kyuh-lur): having strong muscles

pony (POH-nee): a breed of horse that stays small when fully grown

social (SOH-shuhl): preferring to be around others instead of alone

stubborn (STUHB-urn): not willing to give in or change; set on having your own way

Thinking Questions

1. Where are Shetland ponies from?
2. How are Shetland ponies built for living in tough places?
3. What were Shetland ponies once used for? Why?
4. Describe a Shetland pony's personality.
5. What do Shetland ponies eat?

Index

coats 10, 19

colors 11

food 18

kids 4, 15

personality 14, 16, 20

Scotland 6, 7

size 4, 8, 9

strength 9, 12

About the Author

Anne Accardi is a librarian who loves reading books and learning new things! She lives in Kansas City, Missouri. When she's not writing, Anne enjoys listening to music, exploring nature around the city, and spending time with her family.